RADICAL HOLINESS
FOR
RADICAL LIVING

RADICAL HOLINESS
FOR
RADICAL LIVING

C. PETER WAGNER

WAGNER
INSTITUTE
FOR PRACTICAL MINISTRY
Preparing Tomorrow's Church Today

Radical Holiness for Radical Living
Copyright © 1998 by C. Peter Wagner
ISBN 0-9667481-1-5

Published by
Wagner Institute for Practical Ministry
P.O. Box 62958
Colorado Springs, CO 80962-2958

TABLE OF CONTENTS

CHAPTER ONE

WHY IS HOLINESS
A HOT TOPIC?

Several months ago I sensed that God was telling me to raise the subject of holiness to the top of my preaching and teaching agenda. Soon after I began to do this something unusual started to happen.

I have been a public speaker for 50 years. Over those years I have come to realize that I am not considered a particularly outstanding speaker, although I may qualify as slightly above average. The pattern has been that people come up to me after I speak and politely commend me for the message, usually only as a prelude for discussing some issue which I have raised. When we do evaluations of conferences, my ranking by the attendees is rarely, if ever, at the top of the list of the speakers that they heard during the week.

This pattern has changed a bit, however, since I started speaking on holiness. Other messages that I am now doing draw about the same moderate response which I am used to. But when I speak on holiness I get telephone calls, notes in the mail, people stop me in the hallways, all of them expressing incredibly high praise that I "dared" to speak on such a theme. Just recently, for example, I received a note from North Carolina saying, "Your talk tonight on holiness was the most refreshing message I heard all week, and I praise the Lord that He has laid it on your heart to share this for the next few months."

LIFTING THE BANNER OF RADICAL HOLINESS

Naturally, we would ask, "Why?" Why does there seem to be such a hunger out there for lifting the banner of radical holiness? An obvious starting point for answering the question is that it must be something that the Spirit is saying to the churches in our day. Jesus says, "He who has an ear, let him hear what the Spirit says to the churches" (Rev. 2:7).

The whole body of Christ finds itself in a new place in the 1990s, not only here in America but around the world. Never has the Christian church seen such an ongoing harvest of souls, such a dramatic outward manifestation of supernatural power, such a worldwide prayer movement, or such compassion for the poor and needy. We are members of the first generation ever to experience the live possibility of completing the Great Commission of Jesus Christ in our lifetime. But, perhaps most significantly of all, we are seeing the divine government of the church coming into place before our very eyes.

PROPHETS AND APOSTLES ARE WITH US

Many Christians who fervently affirm the trustworthiness and authority of the Bible have all but ignored 40 percent of the Bible verse that says, "[God] Himself gave some to be apostles, some prophets, some evangelists, and some pastors and teachers" (Eph. 4:11). For years we Christians in general have accepted and appreciated the ministry of evangelists, pastors, and teachers. But we have had a very difficult time accepting the ministry of apostles and prophets in our midst. One defensive mechanism has been to relegate such leaders to the "charismatic fringe," and to scorn them as "self-appointed apostles" or "self-appointed prophets." It is very interesting that through all the years, no one has ever called me a "self-appointed teacher!"

Now this widespread phobia against apostles and prophets is melting like an ice cube in a hot frying pan. During the 1980s the gift and office of prophet became widely recognized, and the same thing is happening in the 1990s with the gift and office of apostle. My recent books, *The New Apostolic Churches* and *Churchquake! The Explosive Dynamics of the New Apostolic Reformation* (both published by Regal Books) are helping many Christian leaders understand what is happening in our days. It is not that apostles and prophets have been missing through the centuries, it is just that they are now being recognized and fully released to do what they were appointed by God to do.

NEW SPIRITUAL EQUIPMENT

My interpretation of current events in the Christian world is that our newly-found recognition of prophets and apostles completes the divine government of the church. With the government in place, God is now willing to entrust the body of Christ with revelation, supernatural power, and spiritual equipment that has not previously been known, at least by churches across the board.

This relates directly to fulfilling the Great Commission, as I have mentioned. We are realizing that in the process of spreading the Gospel, especially in the darkest regions of the world which are now coming into light, spiritual warfare is at the very heart of any significant advance of the kingdom. People cannot hear the Gospel because the "god of this age" has blinded their minds (see 2 Cor. 4:3-4). Aggressive spiritual attacks on Satan and his principalities have visibly been paying off. We are finally realizing that winning the air war is a prerequisite for an effective ground war. If the powers of darkness are pushed back through the air war, the ground troops—missionaries, church planters, evangelists, and pastors—will gather in an abundant harvest. No responsible general would send in ground troops without first controlling the air. But the church has been doing this for years and wondering why missionaries come home so battered and beat up.

HOLINESS AND HOLES IN THE ARMOR

The 1990s is the decade, above all others in memory, for aggressive spiritual warfare on the highest levels. One of the things we have learned as we go to the front lines is that we must put on the full armor of God before the battle starts. Paul says, "Put on the whole armor of God, that you may be able to stand against the wiles of the devil" (Eph. 6:11). Most of us try to practice this and we verbally clothe ourselves with truth, the helmet of salvation, the gospel of peace, the sword of the Spirit, and the rest. Teaching on the armor of God abounds.

The individual whom God most used some years ago to introduce my wife, Doris, and me to strategic-level spiritual warfare was Cindy Jacobs, author of *Possessing the Gates of the Enemy* (Chosen Books). Soon after we met her, I heard Cindy say something that I have never forgotten: "We can put on the whole armor of God, but if our hearts are not pure under it, we have holes in our armor!" Satan and his principalities of darkness will be among the first to discover those holes, and we become extremely vulnerable to his fiery darts. The armor of God carries only a one-day warranty, so working on this needs to be a constant and daily part of our lifestyle.

REDUCING THE CASUALTIES

Spiritual warfare is truly *warfare*. Because this is the case, there will always be casualties. But I consider it my role as a leader in this movement and Coordinator of the International Spiritual Warfare Network, to do what I can to reduce the casualties to a minimum. Experience has shown that there are two major causes of casualties in high-level spiritual warfare. One is to miss the timing of God. I deal with that issue in other books. The other cause is lack of holiness, which is why I am writing this book. My prayer is that God will use this book to raise the water level of holiness throughout the body of Christ to the point that our vulnerability to the attacks of the devil will be practically zero.

A Theological Stumbling Block

If I am not mistaken, a major obstacle or stumbling block preventing many believers from living a daily life of holiness according to the plan of God has been the pervasiveness of the Reformed doctrine of holiness or sanctification. My personal theological orientation is Reformed. I was indoctrinated with Reformed theology in both Fuller Theological Seminary and Princeton Theological Seminary during my formative years. It wasn't until I began moving in areas of high-level spiritual warfare not too long ago that I gradually realized that the Reformed doctrine of sanctification was not going to cut it. It became clear that the Wesleyan view of holiness as seen, for example, in the Church of the Nazarene or the Salvation Army or the different branches of Methodism or the Church of God (Anderson, Indiana) or others would provide a much more adequate approach to holiness in terms of helping us to close the holes in our armor.

I was taught that I should strive for holiness, but that I would never make it. If I lived a good Christian life, I could expect to see some progress in my sanctification as I matured in Christ, but I could never be holy because only God is holy. Reformed theology, rooted in the teachings of such as Martin Luther, John Calvin, John Knox, and others, has developed an unsurpassed doctrine of the holiness of God. Holiness as an attribute of God is a very important teaching, although it is not my topic in this book. *Personal* holiness is my topic.

Music directors or worship leaders who know I am going to speak on holiness frequently try to set the stage with having everyone sing what is probably the best-known song on holiness: "Holy, holy, holy, Lord God Almighty; early in the morning my song shall rise to Thee." This is a very meaningful and moving song, but notice that it is a song about the holiness of God, not about our personal holiness. In fact, one phrase in the song clearly reflects what I have been saying about the Reformed doctrine of holiness: "Only Thou art holy." If it is true that only God is holy, it follows that no human being could be holy, in the sense of not committing sin.

I believe that God is holy, but I also believe that you and I can also be holy. 1 Peter 1:15 puts them both together and says, "As He who called you is holy, you also be holy in all your conduct." This is not an unattainable dream, it can be a present-day reality in your life and mine.

CHAPTER TWO

STANDARDS HAVE NOT GONE OUT OF STYLE

I recently read in the newspaper that a certain American judge is engaged in a running battle with his superiors because they want him to take down the Ten Commandments from the wall of his courtroom. In most of the history of our country the idea that the standards expressed in the Ten Commandments should not enter into a judge's decisions would have been regarded as nonsense. No longer. Many people now think that such standards are a thing of the past. The judge is regarded as stubbornly old fashioned.

Much of the Book of James deals with living a holy life. James is very specific about behavior. He says, for example, "If you have bitter envy and self-seeking in your hearts, do not boast and lie against the truth. This wisdom does not descend from above, but is earthly, sensual, demonic" (Jas. 3:14-15). And "Adulterers and adulteresses! Do you not know that friendship with the world is enmity with God? Whoever therefore wants to be a friend of the world makes himself an enemy of God" (Jas. 4:4).

GOD LETS YOU MAKE THE CHOICE

James also says, "Therefore submit to God. Resist the devil and he will flee from you. Draw near to God and He will draw near to you. Cleanse your hands, you sinners; and purify your hearts, you double-minded" (Jas. 4:7-8).

There are four important active verbs in that passage. I say "active," because we have a choice. We can either do them or not. God is not going to do them for us, but He definitely is watching us and hoping that we make the right choices. Living a holy life does not just automatically come with the package of getting saved. It only happens to those who decide that they will do what they know God expects them to do. The active verbs are:

- *Submit* to God
- *Draw near* to God
- *Cleanse* your hands
- *Purify* your hearts

The first two verbs, submit and draw near to God, have to do with relationships. As I will repeat many times, relationships, especially our relationship with God, is the starting point on the road to holiness. The second two verbs, cleanse and purify, have to do with behavior. I think it would be reasonable to assume that "cleanse your hands" refers to our outward behavior that all can see, and "purify your hearts" refers to our inward attitudes. Both are important because they always go together. If *relationships* start the road to holiness, *behavior* carries us to our destination.

How do we go about cleansing our hands and purifying our hearts? How do we reach our destination of a holy life, day in and day out?

- Is it our relationship to God? Yes, this is the starting point, but it is not enough.

- Is it our inward attitude? Yes, we will not be holy without the right attitude, but it takes more.

- Is it the presence of God? Yes, God is a holy God and His presence is essential. But even God's presence is not enough. Take Adam and Eve, for example. There was a time when they were holy and there was a time when they were not holy. God was present both times.

What, then, makes the difference? The difference is adhering to standards. In the Garden of Eden, God set standards for Adam and Eve. It was up to them whether they kept the standards or not. If they had chosen to keep them, the whole human race might have been different. But they chose to violate the standards, and we have been suffering the consequences ever since. My point is, the choice was theirs!

KEEPING FAITH ALIVE

Adam and Eve had faith in God. After all, He came to visit them personally on a regular basis. They knew Him and they talked to Him. Faith in God, which establishes our relationship with Him, is essential to holiness. But faith can be dead. What gives it life? Only proper behavior brings faith to life. That is why God told Adam and Eve that the day they misbehaved, they would surely die. They decided not to obey Him, and even though they still had faith, it became a dead faith. Only obedience could have kept their faith alive.

When it is stated so simply, it is obviously true. That is why James says, "Thus also faith by itself, if it does not have works, is dead. But someone will say, 'You have faith and I have works.' Show me your faith without your works, and I will show you my faith by my works" (Jas. 2:17-18). There are some today who say, "My relationship to God is a personal matter. What I do is between me and Him. You have no right to stand in judgment over my behavior." They are the ones who consider standards as old fashioned.

Saying that standards validate relationships or that works validate faith is strong teaching. It always has been, it always will be. Martin Luther, for example, could not stand it. He, as all of us are, was strongly influenced by his times. But nevertheless, he was so disturbed by James's idea that "faith without works is dead" that in one of his writings Luther declared that James was nothing but "an epistle of straw." Luther apparently thought the New Testament would have been better without James.

IS OUR BEHAVIOR NO ONE ELSE'S BUSINESS?

Luther lived hundreds of years ago. But even today, many will react against the teaching that it is essential to keep standards of behavior in order to please God. For thirteen years I taught the 120 Fellowship Adult Sunday School Class in Lake Avenue Congregational Church in Pasadena, California. Besides teaching in Fuller Seminary and writing books, it was my main grassroots ministry outlet over those years. I had around 100 adults of all ages in the class. I rarely accepted invitations to speak in other churches, because I felt that I needed to be with my people. Since the church had around 5,000 members, the adult Sunday School classes were the places where individual church members found their fellowship and spiritual nurture. I was like their hands-on pastor. I loved to be with them Sunday after Sunday, and they loved me.

The people who chose to come to 120 Fellowship were those who enjoyed being on the cutting edge. I was constantly testing new ideas and experimenting with new forms of ministry with them. We went through many paradigm shifts together and we regarded ourselves as one big family. All went smoothly until I began to teach on holiness over a three-month period. Before I finished, five families had decided to leave the class, and two of them were the two most influential families in the class! That is when it really came home to me that this teaching on standards of behavior as essential for holiness is regarded by some as excessively strong teaching. Those who left did not want the idea of personal holiness pushed farther than affirming our relationship with God. Their behavior was to be regarded as their own business, no one else's.

WE LIVE IN AN AGE OF RELATIVISM

America has entered an age of relativism. Our culture is telling us that if you sincerely believe something is right, it must be right, and others should not criticize. Let the others do what they think is right. Take the Ten Commandments off the wall! Standards are out of style. If this were the attitude of unbelievers only, it would be one thing. But moral relativism has crept into our churches as well.

Today's best known church researcher is George Barna. He is a committed Christian, but his task is that of a sociologist, not of a moralizer. Keep that in mind when you read this quote from his recent book *The Second Coming of the Church*: "The Bible clearly states that true believers should be readily distinguished from nonbelievers by the way they live. Yet, the evidence undeniably suggests that most American Christians today do not live in a way that is quantifiably different from their non-Christian peers, in spite of the fact that they profess to believe in a set of principles that should clearly set them apart."[1]

How is this mindset expressed? I am going to quote one of America's highly-visible Christian youth leaders, but I am not going to mention the name. My purpose is not to embarrass an individual, but to quote what is taken as common currency, especially among believers born after 1965. Any number of others would agree when they read it. This leader says that teenagers today "think personal holiness is living up to a standard, and they either get frustrated and give up or lower the standard, so they can feel more comfortable." So if holiness does not involve honoring standards, what is it all about? He goes on, "They rarely understand that personal holiness *is not external behavior,* but an intimate relationship with Jesus born out of God's grace." There is no problem in the minds of many Christians in separating *be lief* from *behavior.*

This is exactly what Barna is finding. To put it in other terminology, Barna has found that Christians score high on faith. They believe in God the Father Almighty, maker of heaven and earth, and in Jesus Christ, His only Son, our Lord." But they score low on works. What would James say about this? Since faith without works is dead, what we are seeing is obviously not a very vigorous faith. We live in a Christian culture that majors on belief but minors on behavior. I believe that things would be different in our country if every judge and every school teacher and the President and members of the cabinet each posted the Ten Commandments on their walls and took the pains to read them from time to time!

WHAT IS HOLINESS?

The Greek word for holy is *hagios.* Its root meaning is "to be set apart." It carries two nuances: set apart *from* and set apart *to.* The predominant emphasis in the New Testament is that we are set apart *to God.* But this does not preempt the important issue of what we are set apart *from.* According to George Barna's research, American Christians today are not set apart from much of anything. But, deep down, they know that they should be. Realizing this is probably a chief reason why so many Christians today are hungry to hear a message or to read a book on holiness. In their heart of hearts they know that standards have not gone out of style.

[1] George Barna, *The Second Coming of the Church* (Nashville TN: Word Publishing, 1998), pp. 120-121.

CHAPTER THREE

BIBLICAL HOLINESS IS RADICAL HOLINESS

Holiness is a godly quality that we cannot internalize without a fundamental understanding of what the Bible has to say about it. Since standards have not gone out of style, and since we have a deep need to know what the standards for our life are, where do we find those standards? Do we seek a human leader and expect the leader to set standards? If so, we might end up with a Joseph Stalin or an Adolph Hitler. Do we take a vote and agree that the consensus of the majority sets the standards? We've tried that and ended up with mass abortions, homosexuality as an alternate lifestyle, and the breakdown of the nuclear family.

We Christians might live in a political system which operates on human standards, but we are also supposed to be "set apart," which, as I have explained, is the root meaning of "holy." Our standards come from our Creator, our Lord, and our Savior. They are written in the Word of God, the Bible. Whatever the Bible says we're supposed to do, we do because we know that is God's ideal design for our lives. Following the Bible's standards might make us appear to be countercultural, which, in this day and age, may not be such a bad thing. It is impossible for you and me to be everything that God wants us to be without knowing and following God's standards. And if we do it consistently, we will surely be seen as radical!

God's standards of holiness are not something that we have to ferret out in some obscure passages of Scripture. They are clear and plain and unambiguous. And they are repeated over and over again, both in the Old Testament and in the New Testament. In this chapter, I am going to touch on a couple of the highpoints so that we can fix in our minds the idea that biblical holiness is, indeed, radical holiness.

LEGALISM VS. LICENTIOUSNESS

The Apostle Paul wrote the entire book of Galatians to help the believers in the churches of that area understand how to live a holy Christian life. In order to get his point across, Paul had to do a balancing act because he was writing to two very different groups of believers, the Jews and the Gentiles.

The Jewish believers had come to Christ out of a background of obedience. They had been taught since childhood that they were required to obey God's law, and they brought this mindset into the church. On the other hand, the Gentile believers came out of a background of licentiousness. Everything goes! If it feels good, do it!

Throughout the book of Galatians, Paul goes back and forth and addresses both groups. The Jews needed to understand that their godly behavior would be based on their *relationships*. Paul tells them that the law was given as "our tutor to bring us to Christ" (Gal. 3:24), and that we have become "sons of God through faith in Christ Jesus" (Gal. 3:26). The more the Jewish believers could understand that, the more liberty they would find in their new Christian life.

RIGHT AND WRONG

But the Gentile believers didn't need more liberty. Just the opposite. They needed to learn *obedience*. Being Christlike involves moral standards. It was important that they know the difference between right and wrong. In Galatians 5 Paul is very clear about this. The wrong things are called "the works of the flesh" including adultery, licentiousness, idolatry, drunkenness, and hatred, just to mention a few (see Gal. 5:19-21). The right things are called "the fruit of the Spirit" including love, kindness, faithfulness, gentleness, and self-control, just to name a few of them (see Gal. 5:22-23).

Realizing that his teaching would cause a certain amount of tension, Paul tries to resolve it in Gal. 5:13: "For you, brethren [this part is for the Jews], have been called to liberty; only [this part is for the Gentiles] do not use liberty as an opportunity for the flesh."

CHILDREN *AND* SLAVES

The Jews needed to realize that God was their *Father*, (relationship!) and that they were children and heirs of God. The Gentiles needed to realize that God was their *Master* and that they were His slaves. Both are true, and neither one should be either underemphasized or overemphasized. But Paul explains the way that this works out in real life: "Now I say that the heir as long as he is a child does not differ at all from a slave, though he is master of all" (Gal. 4:1). What does this mean to us today? It means that we have an incredible family-type relationship to God Almighty and that we possess a divine inheritance. But day-by-day we relate to God as children are supposed to relate to their natural fathers, and obedience to the Father's will, including His standards, is not up for discussion. It is *required*.

Suppose we choose to be disobedient and to violate the Father's standards? We are in trouble! Switching to Hebrews for a moment, we are told to "pursue ... holiness, without which no one will see the Lord" (Heb. 12:14). This passage in Hebrews 12 mentions that we are sons twelve times, so there is no question as to the relationship. However, if we are truly children of the Father, we can expect that disobedience will involve punishment. "For what son is there whom a father does not chasten [punish]? (Heb. 12:7). "For whom the Lord loves, He chastens" (Heb. 12:6). Why does God punish us? He does it "for our profit, that we may be partakers of His holiness" (Heb. 12:10). Notice how important our holiness is in the mind of God. He knows that if we choose to obey Him, we will prosper in every way.

RELATIONSHIPS ALWAYS HAVE STANDARDS

A desire to honor standards is an essential part of any close human relationship. Most of us understand it. For example, my most important human relationship is with my wife, Doris. Soon after we got married, I found that she has certain standards. I experimented once or twice in violating those standards, and I found myself in deep trouble. It happened the other way around also, because I came into the marriage with my personal standards as well. Neither one of us wanted to live around a spouse who was feeling violated and wounded. So it didn't take us long to decide that we would honor each other's standards. One of the benefits of that decision was that, at this writing, we are getting ready to celebrate our 48th wedding anniversary!

Now, how about our relationship to God? Are there parallels? There certainly are. I must say that the statement of the youth leader I quoted in the last chapter to the effect that our intimacy with Christ counts, but following standards does not count makes no sense to me. God has given us His word so that we would know what His standards are. How can we maintain a loving relationship without honoring the standards of the person we love? It won't work in a marriage and it won't work with our Lord.

DELINEATING THE STANDARDS

The Bible is not vague on this subject of standards. In fact, every one of the three or four substantial New Testament passages on holiness delineates specifically what holy people *do* and what they do *not* do.

Take, for example, Colossians 3, a chapter on holiness. In the middle of the chapter, verse 12, it speaks of the elect of God, "*holy* and beloved." Preceding this verse is a list of 12 things that holy people do not do, and following it are 12 things that holy people do.

To be specific, holy people avoid fornication, uncleanness, passion, evil desire, covetousness, idolatry, anger, wrath, malice, blasphemy, filthy language, and lying. Holy people are characterized by tender mercy, kindness, humility, meekness, longsuffering, forgiveness, love, peace, thankfulness, marital harmony, obedient children, and working for a living.

These lists are extremely practical. Hardly any believer in Christ would ever say that they would choose to do the bad things in the first list and that they didn't want to be characterized by the good things in the second list.

Avoiding Legalism

Stressing these standards should not be interpreted as legalism. Legalism has been a very large problem in the body of Christ in recent generations. In Chapter One, I argued that the Wesleyan understanding of holiness is more useful for us than the Reformed viewpoint. Unfortunately, however, many of the denominations that based their doctrine of holiness on Wesleyan theology around the turn of the century, allowed their practice to degenerate into legalism. They got to the point where they would evaluate a person's holiness on whether or not they kept certain rules. In most cases holiness was gained by abstaining from such things as make up, movies, slacks on women, dancing, alcoholic beverages, card playing, jewelry, and the like.

Understandably, when the "holiness movement" became associated primarily with this sort of legalism, many good-hearted believers chose to distance themselves from it. Ironically, the legalism perpetrated by many holiness denominations has probably been as much of a stumbling block to the practice of biblical holiness across the body of Christ as has the Reformed doctrine of sanctification. Fortunately, many of the holiness denominations would now agree with what I have said, and they have been modifying their practices. The door is now open for Christians in general, across the theological spectrum, to choose the kind of radical holiness which is authentically biblical.

CHAPTER FOUR

THE TEST OF HOLINESS: OBEDIENCE

How do you know if you're holy? Very simple: you are obeying the standards of Jesus Christ!

This is far different from checking to see if you are following a set of rules developed by a legalistic denomination. It is based on your relationship to God. Here is the way the Bible describes this test: "Now by this we know that we know Him [our relationship], if we keep His commandments" (1 Jn. 2:3). It would make no sense to say, "I love God, but I don't love Him enough to do what He wants me to do." That is why John goes on and says, "He who says 'I know Him,' and does not keep His commandments, is a liar, and the truth is not in him" (1 Jn. 2:4).

"OBEDIENCE" IS NOT A POPULAR WORD

The social psychology of the United States took an interesting turn after World War II. The war was fought against dictators: Hitler, Mussolini, and Hirohito. It was such a traumatic experience for the nation that we collectively decided that we as a people wanted nothing to do with dictatorship. Partly as a result of this, an anti-authority strain began to permeate our national thinking. For example, colleges began teaching "Maslow's Hierarchy." Maslow had suggested that human needs were like a pyramid with basic survival needs at the bottom, and other needs rising to the apex of the pyramid which was "self-actualization." Practically a whole generation accepted self-actualization as a life goal. But notice what this implies. If I am self-actualized, I really don't need you. I am my own final authority. My ultimate obedience is to myself. I don't need to obey you or anyone else.

Should Wives Obey Husbands?

That is when "obedience" began to become an unpopular word. To illustrate, a funny thing happened in the 1960s. When men and women from previous generations got married, most of the wedding vows routinely included the wife's promise to *obey* her husband. That was simply considered the proper thing to do in those generations. It was commonly accepted as an application of Ephesians 5:22-25 which says that wives should submit to husbands. The husbands did not reciprocally promise to "obey" our wives, but we both promised to "love" our wives in an attempt to apply Ephesians 5:25, "Husbands, love your wives."

However, in the current generations born after 1945, most brides have decided to take the word "obey" out of their wedding vows on the grounds of equality. It is the exception, not the rule, for wives to promise to obey their husbands. Obedience has become unpopular, and hardly anyone in our generations is willing to promise to obey. The result? Look at what has happened to the divorce rate in our country beginning in the 1960s!

As I grew up and became an adult, I had my share of problems. But it never occurred to me to blame my problems on my parents. One of the most common things among the current generation is to blame their troubles on their parents. The pre-World War II generation *obeyed* their parents, while the post-World War

II generation *objected to* their parents.

DYSFUNCTIONAL FAMILIES AND DYSFUNCTIONAL CHURCHES

All this is tied to our obedience to Christ, as it says in Ephesians 5:24, "Just as the church is subject to Christ, so let the wives be subject to their husbands in everything." If we choose not to obey, not only in our marriages but also in other aspects of our life, we end up with dysfunctional families and also dysfunctional churches.

Take Vineyard Christian Fellowship as an example. This was a church founded toward the end of the 1970s, and built on the post-World War II generation. By the time it was ten years old, it had grown phenomenally, but obedience had not become a high value among the members.

The issue revolved around overemphasizing relationship and underemphasizing obedience, a very sensitive issue among baby boomers. The good news was the deep desire among those in Vineyard to develop intimacy with the Father. Vineyard worship music became popular in churches across America as "love songs to God." But the bad news was that God's blessing had begun to lift off the church. There was an above average number of moral failures, even among the staff. John Wimber, the founder, began to feel low and burnt out.

That was when God brought Vineyard in contact with Mike Bickle and the "Kansas City prophets." They issued a strong and urgent call to obedience. Vineyard convened its first conference on holiness in February 1990, and their people were so hungry for holiness that it sold out with 4,500 in attendance, and they had to schedule another one the following week to accommodate another 4,500.

Vineyard's problem was not too much legalism, but much too much licentiousness. The focus had become "what God does for me," not "what I do for God." They had been trying to maintain a relationship without honoring the standards which flowed from the relationship. It didn't work. Never has, never will!

THE POWER TO OBEY

If our relationship to Jesus is validated by our obedience, how can we do this? Where do we get the power to obey? Paul wrote Romans 7 and 8 to explain that our obedience to Jesus cannot be accomplished through the flesh, but only by the power of the Holy Spirit. Trying to obey in the flesh will lead to the kind of desperation that Paul felt: "O wretched man that I am! Who will deliver me from this body of death?" (Rom. 7:24). But the release comes in Romans 8:1: "There is therefore now no condemnation to those who are in Christ Jesus, who do not walk according to the flesh, but according to the Spirit."

The only way to sustain an authentic life of holiness is to be filled with the Holy Spirit. I know that there are different views about the filling of the Holy Spirit, but mine is that we need to be refilled every day. I base it on the implications of "Be not drunk with wine . . . but be filled with the Holy Spirit" (Eph. 5:18). As any drunk can tell you, drunkenness lasts only one day. You may get drunk today, but if you want to be drunk tomorrow, you will have to get drunk again. Apparently, the filling of the Holy Spirit is similar. Because of that, I ask the Lord to fill me with the Holy Spirit every morning, and I believe He does, because Jesus said that if a son asks his father for bread he will not give him a stone. The same applies in asking the heavenly Father for the Holy Spirit (see Luke 11:13).

This is very important for a life of holiness. Part of the package of being filled with the Holy Spirit is that He convicts the world of sin, righteousness, and judgment (see Jn. 16:8). This means that the Holy Spirit will see that you keep on the road of holiness by convicting you if you begin going astray. Think how reassuring this can be. If you are filled with the Holy Spirit, the possibility emerges that you can actually live a holy life, free from sin, day after day.

I want to look at that in detail in the next chapter.

CHAPTER FIVE

IT CAN BE DONE!

Is it possible to be holy? If it were not, I can assure you that I wouldn't be writing this book. I am radical enough to believe that you and I can actually live lives without sin, day in and day out!

TWO QUESTIONS AND ANSWERS

Let's begin by putting it in the shape of two questions and answers that will clarify many things for us:

- Can anyone be holy? Yes. As a matter of fact, in one way of looking at it, every Christian is holy.

- Can anyone be holy enough? No. No Christian is ever holy enough.

As I have pointed out, the root meaning of "holy," or "*hagios,*" is to be set apart. Anything set apart to God is considered holy.

That is why the Bible speaks of such things as a holy city or holy prophets or holy law or a holy kiss and so on. In the broadest sense, therefore, every true Christian is holy, set apart to God. Peter says we are "a royal priesthood, a holy nation" (1 Peter 2:9). We get there by being born again and becoming members of God's family. The Bible frequently refers to believers as "saints," and that word comes from *hagios*, literally "holy ones." When we become Christians we are set apart *from* the world, we are different from non-Christians, and we are set apart *to* God and His family. That is the sense in which we can say that every Christian is holy.

CHRISTIANS DO NOT SIN

Let's look at two scriptures which, at first glance, may appear to be contradictory. The first is 1 John 3:6: "Whoever abides in Him does not sin. Whoever sins has neither seen Him nor known Him."

What does this mean? It means that true believers no longer live a lifestyle that is characterized by sinning. Those who have been raised in Christian families and who have had a relatively smooth pathway into the church may not understand this very well. But those of us, myself included, who at one time were adult non-Christians, totally outside the church, know exactly what it means. When we are born again we become new creatures in Christ. The old things—the lifestyle characterized by sin—pass away. All things become new—a totally new lifestyle characterized by not sinning. What a difference! My life has never been the same, meaning in part that I no longer do or want to do many things that I used to do before I was saved.

This is characteristic of my circle of Christian friends also. I can't think of a single Christian person whom I regularly hang out with that goes around sinning, and I am associated with a large number of them. True, there may be some who are sinning secretly, but if they are they had better double check to see if they are really saved. At least that is what 1 John 3:6 implies.

CHRISTIANS SIN

I purposely made the two last sub-titles sound like a contradiction: "Christians Do Not Sin," and "Christians Sin." Christians may live a lifestyle separated from sin, but that does not mean that they cannot or never do sin. They do! Here is what 1 John 1:8 says: "If we say that we have no sin, we deceive ourselves and the truth is not in us."

This is why I have said that no Christian can be holy enough. Only when we get to heaven will we be totally free from the possibility of sin coming into our life. Meanwhile, sin does get in. So what do we do? Do we just say, "Well, that's the way the mop flops! I'm going to sin from time to time, so I may as well get used to it because no one's perfect!" No! If we truly know God, we hate sin and we deal with it aggressively. If we are on the road to radical holiness, we will reject the "qué será, será" mentality.

Here is what we do: (1) we deal with the sin and confess it immediately, and (2) we take steps to see that sin invades our lives as infrequently as possible, and that the rule of our life is to live without sinning. Sin, then, becomes the clear exception to the rule for us. The rule is living a holy life. Let me explain.

I HAVEN'T SINNED!

I am writing this in the evening, and so far today I have not sinned.

To be honest, I didn't expect to sin today, nor do I expect to sin before I go to bed tonight. In fact, I did not sin yesterday. Not that I couldn't have sinned yesterday or that there is no possibility that I may sin before I go to bed tonight, but so far so good.

Every morning, without fail, I take preventative measures. The way I do it is by praying the Lord's prayer. By this I don't mean that I *say* the Lord's prayer, but that I *pray* the Lord's prayer. I learned to do this from Larry Lea years ago. He brought to my attention the fact that on two separate occasions when the disciples asked Jesus to explain to them how they should pray, He gave them what we now call the Lord's prayer. One of these occasions is in Matthew and one in Luke, but they are not parallel passages. They were 1 ½ years apart. I have not found any more useful framework for daily praying than the Lord's prayer.

FORGIVE MY SINS

Every morning, therefore, I say to God, "Please forgive my sins as I forgive those who sin against me." I think these are the best words, rather than the archaic words "debts" or "trespasses." When I do this, I have trained myself to take a mental review of the past 24 hours to see if I have done anything that I need to confess. This morning I came up blank, and that is why I came to the conclusion that I didn't sin yesterday.

How do I know that I didn't make a mistake and that I really *did* sin yesterday? It is because I am filled with the Holy Spirit. As I explained in the last chapter, one of the roles of the Holy Spirit in our lives is to convict us of sin. If I had sinned, the Holy Spirit would have brought it to my mind. This is why I make sure that every morning I also ask God to fill me with the Holy Spirit.

When it comes right down to it, if we are filled with the Holy Spirit, we don't ordinarily have to wait until the next morning to discover that we sinned yesterday. In my case, when I do sin, I know it right on the spot. The Holy Spirit leaves no question in my mind. And I usually confess it instantly. I say "usually" because not too long ago, the Holy Spirit convicted me of a sin, but I stayed in denial for about two hours. That evasive attempt didn't work, the Holy Spirit kept my feet to the fire, and I finally confessed it.

I must admit that I usually confess sins like this again the next morning just to make sure. I realize that this is really not necessary because when we confess our sins, God forgives us and our sin is put away from us as far as the east is from the west. I don't necessarily recommend it for you, but I do it anyhow.

LEAD ME NOT INTO TEMPTATION

The next thing I ask the Lord is, "Lead me not into temptation." And I guess it goes without saying that I expect God to answer my prayer. If He does, and if I go through the whole day without being tempted, I have no reason to expect to sin.

I realize that some will read this and wonder where I am coming from. To them it is impossible to go a whole day without sinning. Some have made a distinction between sins of *commission* and sins of *omission*. If they can't think of any sin they have committed, they conclude that there must be things that they should have done or done better, so they confess that. Without realizing it, they are confusing *perfection* with *holiness*. We can be holy, but we cannot be perfect. The song, "Holy, Holy, Holy" is correct when it says that only God is "perfect in power, in love, and purity."

I know a family that routinely confesses their sins at every meal and also before they go to bed. To be honest, I think that too much confession, not only privately but even in our church services, can tend to trivialize sin. Why assume on Sunday morning, for example, that everyone who has come to church has sinned during the past week? If we can be holy for a day, can't we be holy for a week? I would expect that in a healthy church, the assumption would be that we *haven't* sinned, or that at least if we have, we have confessed it at the time we sinned, rather than waiting for the next church service.

When I affirm that we can be *holy*, but that we can't be *perfect*, let's not make that a cop-out. I recently heard a Christian leader say, "Nobody is perfect! Everyone has sin issues that they are dealing with." I would agree that no one is perfect. But I don't think that this gives us an excuse to put up with a "sin issue" in our lives, and expect it to continue. If there is a "sin issue" today, we should deal with it decisively and not have it continuing tomorrow. We then can say, "I *had* a sin issue," and not, "I *have* a sin issue."

DELIVER ME FROM THE EVIL ONE

As a final reinforcement, Jesus instructs us to pray, "Deliver me [or us] from the Evil One." The older language, "deliver us from evil," often causes us to miss the point that we are praying protection from the devil. When I pray this, I again expect God to answer. If He does keep me from Satan, I will not be tempted because God does not tempt people (see James 1:13). It is the devil who tries to get me to yield to my own desires and to sin.

Holiness is not some evasive and unrealistic goal. If it were, God wouldn't command us to be holy, and expect us to obey His command. Can it be done? Yes, it can be done!

CHAPTER SIX

MEASURING YOUR HOLINESS

If we can be holy, and if holiness of life becomes our goal, how can we measure our progress? Can I be holier and holier as time goes on? Can I be more holy this year than I was last year? I think the answer is "yes." Admittedly it might be a bit difficult to measure it on an annual basis, but I think I can accurately say that I am more holy in 1998 than I was in 1988, ten years ago. How do I know? Because I see more fruit of the Spirit in my life now, and others confirm it to me.

THE DANGER OF VISIBLE INDICATORS

As we progress in our holiness there has often been a temptation to set up visible indicators to help measure our progress. This is like the "foolish Galatians" who were going back to the law (see Gal. 3:1). We should avoid the trap of letting legalism define our holiness. Even thinking that some form of a "second blessing" that we might have experienced sometime in the past has made us "holy enough" is a danger.

The picture begins to come together when we balance *direction* with *accomplishment*. The direction, or our inward holiness, is first and foremost. Who knows if I really have a clean heart? People close to me know—my spouse, my children, my close colleagues, my prayer partners. If my direction is right, then my outward accomplishments will follow. I will go to church, I will pray, I will tithe my income, I will maintain high morality, and I will abstain from ungodly activities, just to mention a few of the more obvious behavior traits. But these accomplishments cannot *prove* that I am holy, as the Pharisees soon found out. The Pharisees strictly kept the law (accomplishments), but they were far from God (direction).

THE VALUE OF OUTWARD ACCOMPLISHMENTS

If our inward direction takes precedence over our outward accomplishments, which it does, then what good are outward standards of behavior? This is an important question that many will ask. There are at least three answers to that question:

1. Outward standards help reveal the *absence* of holiness.
Even though your outward actions cannot prove that you *are* holy, some of them certainly can prove that you *aren't* holy! You know what they are, God knows what they are, and your friends know what they are. Enough said!

2. Standards can reflect degrees of Christian maturity.
God is our Father, He is patient, and He understands spiritual children. We begin our Christian journey as babes in Christ, but God expects us to grow up. We do the same with our own children. One way to scold our five-year-old child is to say, "You're acting like you were two!" Or, "Act your age!"

For example, Paul was really upset with the Corinthian believers because they weren't acting their age. He says to them: "I, brethren, could not speak to you as spiritual people but as to carnal, as to babes in Christ" (1 Cor. 3:1). There was no question that they were true believers and that they had a relationship to God, but their outward behavior was childlike.

This happened recently in real life with the Vineyard Christian Fellowship which John Wimber was pastoring. By 1989 they were more than ten years old, but they were acting like they were three. That is when Wimber began to build relationships with Paul Cain, Mike Bickle and the Kansas City Prophets, as I mentioned in Chapter 4. *Christianity Today* reported that "Wimber credits [Paul] Cain's ministry with saving the Vineyard."[1]

What was going on? Keep in mind that Paul Cain is one of America's most respected prophets. "Cain told [Wimber] that God stood ready to forgive the sins of the Vineyard, that Wimber was to take a more authoritative and directive role, and that he was no longer to tolerate 'loose living and low standards,' but was to emphasize holiness."[2] He might as well have said, "Vineyard, act your age!" Happily, Wimber and his church obeyed the word of the Lord, and they have been better off ever since.

3. Standards are requirements for Christian leadership.
The moment a believer accepts the role of a leader in the body of Christ, they move to a higher level of responsibility and accountability before God. James 3:1 says: "My brethren, let not many of you become teachers, knowing that we shall receive a stricter judgment." God evidently has a double standard of judgment, one for leaders and one for the rest.

The Bible does not give us a list of behavioral requirements for maintaining church membership. For example, Paul wrote 1 Corinthians to a church involved in division, law suits with each other, marital problems, drunkenness at the Lord's Supper, disorderly services, eating idol meat, rebellious women, abuse of tongues, and heresy on the doctrine of the resurrection. But he recommended excommunication for only one church member— the one who was living in open immorality with his stepmother.

The situation changes radically for leaders. There are detailed lists of behavioral requirements for bishops, deacons, deacons' wives, and elders (or pastors). If an individual does not live up to those standards, they can remain as members of the church, but they cannot be a leader.

This means that if you are a pastor or on a church staff or a cell group leader or a deacon or an elder or a trustee or a Sunday School teacher or a ministry leader or a worship leader or a seminary professor or a denominational executive or an evangelist, just to name a few, living a holy life is not an option. It is a requirement.

LEADERS DERIVE INFLUENCE FROM HOLINESS

My biblical role model is the Apostle Paul. I want to be like Paul when I grow up! One reason that Paul was such an influential leader was that he practiced living a holy life. When he wrote his rebuke to the Corinthians, he was able to say to them: "I know nothing against myself" (1 Cor. 4:4). This means that Paul examined his heart, searched his inner being before God, and found nothing unholy there. Because he was pure, he could go on to say, "Therefore I urge you, imitate me" (1 Cor. 4:16).

I try to do the same thing. When I am teaching my classes in Fuller Seminary, I am the leader. I, therefore, stand in front of my students and say, "Do you want to know how to live the Christian life? Live it like I live it! Do you want to know to relate to your spouse? Relate like I do! Do you want to know how to raise your kids or pay your income tax or give your tithes and offerings or use your time or what to eat or drink or what to watch on television? Look at the way I do it, and do the same!"

Now, this could sound like pure arrogance. I understand that. But, when it comes right down to it, what other option do I have? What else could I say to my students? If I can't tell them to imitate me, I disqualify myself as their leader. Oh, I might be able to teach them enough to pass an exam, but I cannot be their *leader*.

Please don't misunderstand me. I am not saying that I am perfect. I am not saying that others do not treat their spouses better or raise their kids better or have a better diet than I do. I don't see myself as the best or as holier-than-thou. But what I am saying is that in my outward behavior, I do follow God's standards day in and day out. And I recommend the same for you!

Our leadership is validated by our character. And our behavior invariably reflects our true character.

FOUR NON-NEGOTIABLE PRINCIPLES FOR RADICAL HOLINESS

If at this point you are saying, "I love God and I want to follow His standards," here is a checklist of four non-negotiable principles for a life of radical holiness:

1. Be sure you are in a proper relationship to God.

First of all, be sure you are born again. I assume that almost every reader of a book like this will be born again, but if not, ask your pastor or a good Christian friend to help you. Secondly, be sure you are in daily contact with God. Your holy life is based on a relationship, and a relationship needs daily contact. No matter where I travel in the world, I call my wife every day because that is my most important human relationship. God is my most important relationship of all, so I make sure I contact Him every day.

Note that I said a *proper* relationship, not a *perfect* relationship. God knows your heart and He knows if your true heart desire is to know Him and please Him.

2. Confess all known sins.

God will forgive any and all of your sins, but not if you don't specifically confess them. If you have any doubt as to what may be a sin, review Galatians 5:19-21 and Colossians 3:5-9 and the Ten Commandments and other biblical lists of sins. If anything on those lists is true of you, get rid of it immediately!

While you do this, do not indulge in spiritual self-flagellation. Don't repeat confessing old sins that have already been forgiven. Don't make up sins just to have something to confess. Trust the Holy Spirit to convict you of your real unconfessed sins in an unmistakable way.

At the same time, don't make the mistake of rationalizing guilt away. In other words, suppose you and your friend are having premarital sex. You say to each other, "Well, everybody's doing it and we really love each other, so it must be o.k." It definitely is possible to sear your own conscience to such an extent that you build a barrier to the work of the Holy Spirit in convicting you of the sin. If so, you cannot possibly be the person God wants you to be until you get out of denial and face reality. Confess the sin and agree with your partner that "true love waits." The same thing applies to whatever else you are doing that you know, down deep, is violating God's standard.

Once you do this, be sure that you do whatever is necessary to repair whatever damage your sin may have caused.

3. Seek healing for persistent sin patterns.

It is an unfortunate fact of life that the devil actively rallies his troops to prevent God's people from being holy. He would much rather see the church filled with sin and carnality than to be characterized by holiness.

Satan does not get away with all that he desires because greater is He that is in us than he that is in the world. Nevertheless, it is possible that he may get through to us from time to time, using the world, the flesh and the devil.

Here is how it plays out in some cases. You know that your heart is right and your desire is to please God in everything. You confess a sin and you are forgiven. But a couple of days later it is back. This doesn't just happen once, but over and over again. You are frustrated because you are finding yourself doing things that you do not want to do. In other words, you are out of control. Something else seems to be controlling you and it is obviously not God.

What I have just described are common symptoms of demonization. This is a spiritual illness that needs healing just as much as bodily illnesses such as bladder infections or stomach ulcers or diabetes. You will usually need outside help for this healing. I say "usually" because self-deliverance is possible in many cases. For some just understanding who you really are in Christ will do it, and the sin pattern will evaporate. But in many other cases it won't. This is like having a stomach ache and taking Alka-Seltzer or Pepto Bismol. It frequently does the trick. But when it doesn't, you decide to see a specialist. Increasingly, there are those who are specialized in getting rid of demons in our churches today, and they should be sought out by those with persistent sin problems.

4. Allow others to read your spiritual barometer.
Relate closely to one or more other people whose spirituality you respect and who know you and love you well enough to be open and frank with you, and you with them. Some home cell groups fill this need. Sometimes it is a personal friend. Doris and I have a very close circle of twenty-two I-1 and I-2 intercessors (using the terminology of my book, *Prayer Shield*) who hear from God about us and to whom we have given God permission to tell everything about our lives. As a result, we realize that it is impossible for us to have secrets They use the information well because they love us and pray for us. Without their ministry, we would have a very difficult time living the holy lives that we desire.

CONCLUSION

You and I can do it! We can be the people that God really wants us to be. God is holy and we can be holy. It is our choice. We can live a radical life for God by choosing to be radically holy. My prayer is that you will say, "Yes, God," and do whatever it takes to make it happen!

---

[1]Michael G. Maudlin, "Seers in the Heartland," *Christianity Today,* January 14, 1991, p. 21.
[2] Ibid.

What is
Global Harvest Ministries?

There are still two billion individuals who are not within reach of the gospel and who do not yet have a vital, indigenous church movement.
Global Harvest Ministries, under the leadership of Dr. C. Peter Wagner, unites existing national and international prayer networks in order to focus maximum prayer power on world evangelization; especially for the lost people of the 10/40 Window.

Working with Christian leaders all over the earth, Global Harvest is **seeking to bring together a massive prayer force** that is equipped, trained and focused for the fierce spiritual battles that will free millions of people from the grip of the enemy, and allow them to hear and receive the Gospel.

We are seeking those who will join hands with us in the following ways:

- **In Prayer:** Mobilizing intercession and prayer for the world's most spiritually impoverished peoples.

- **With Financial Help:** Monthly support is needed to mobilize this massive, worldwide prayer effort.

If you are interested in helping in these ways, or would like more information on Global Harvest Ministries please contact us at:

Global Harvest Ministries
P.O. Box 63060
Colorado Springs, CO 80962-3060
Phone: 719-262-9922
E-Mail: Info@globalharvest.org
Web Site: www.globalharvest.org

WAGNER
I N S T I T U T E
F O R   P R A C T I C A L   M I N I S T R Y

Preparing Tomorrow's Church Today

The Wagner Institute for Practical Ministry was initiated in 1997 to be a catalyst to "Prepare Tomorrow's Church Today."

The Institute is being built from the ground up to provide quality training for practical ministry. The emphasis is not just on events, but on a process that will lead to realistic implementation of the training provided.

Our goal is to see each member of the body of Christ fully empowered and functioning in their giftings and callings. We are committed to excellence by providing the body with well-known leaders who will target training in key issues for the Church.

Dr. C. Peter Wagner

Please contact us for a full list of resources, upcoming conferences, and services that will help equip you to fulfill the Lord's call on your life:

Wagner Institute
P.O. Box 62958
Colorado Springs, CO 80962-2958
Phone: 719-262-0442
E-mail: admin@cpwagner.net
Web Site: www.cpwagner.net

The World Prayer Center, located in Colorado Springs, is the international coordination center for a growing movement of people dedicated to praying for the good news of Jesus Christ to go forth into every nation, every tribe, every community in the world. Built with state-of-the-art computer and tele-communications systems, the World Prayer Center is designed specifically for people to pray. It is equipped with computers, telephones, fax machines, e-mail and other communication technology to serve the body of Christ with informative and timely prayer notices. The World Prayer Center connects globally with prayer partners and prayer room networks who are dedicated to push into the invisible world for the lost

Linking Up With the World Prayer Center

There are two ways for direct electronic linkage with the World Prayer Center, and through us with intercessors and prayer movements around the world. Here they are:

1. **National Prayer Networks.** If you live in a country other than the U.S.A., your contact with the World Prayer Center will be through a National Prayer Network. For information on National Prayer Networks, please contact:

**Rich Danzeisen
World Prayer Center
11005 Hwy. 83, #119
Colorado Springs, CO 80921
Phone: 719-262-9922 Fax: 719-262-9920
E-Mail: RDanzeisen@wpccs.org**

2. **Local Church Prayer Rooms.** The World Prayer Center serves as the National Prayer Network for the U.S.A. While we will be linking up with the headquarters of the major prayer ministries in our country, the principal way for any interested individual to link to the World Prayer Center is

through their local church prayer room. This opens up the possibility for every congregation in America to move into a new level of prayer for their church family, for their community, and for the world.

What is a local church prayer room? It begins when a church of any denomination decides to designate a physical room in their church facility exclusively to prayer. They furnish it and decorate it comfortably and tastefully. They install at least one telephone line, although some have two or three. They install a fax machine and a computer with modems for email and Internet. They put an individual with gifts for prayer and intercession, combined with some organizational skills, in charge. This prayer room leader recruits a volunteer staff which will occupy the prayer room up to 24 hours per day, 7 days a week.

Naturally, most of the prayer requests will come from their own congrega-tion, their own community, and even from other churches in the commu-nity. But they will  also be linked, through the World Prayer Center, with thousands of other local church prayer rooms in all states and with the National Prayer Networks around the world.

If you are interested in applying for membership in the Prayer Room Network or in receiving more information, please contact:

Bobbye Byerly
World Prayer Center
11005 Hwy. 83, #119
Colorado Springs, CO 80921
Phone: 719-262-9922 Fax: 719-262-9920
E-Mail: BByerly@wpccs.org